TOP SECRET

CLASSIFIED

BELONGS TO:

____